The Prodigal Daughter Returns

A Song of Restoration and Redemption

Brick,
Thank you so much for your support! Words can never express how much your friendship means to me! All the best,

Keshu

MaKelia D. Mitchell, Ph.D.

Published by The DOCMDM Publishing and Writing Works, LLC

Requests for information should be addressed to: THEDOCMDM@GMAIL.COM

Printed in the United States of America

ISBN - 978-1-7336118-0-0

Library of Congress No. 2019900980

Published by The DOCMDM Publishing and Writing Works, LLC, Largo, MD

Edited by The Comprehensive Editing, Writing & Publishing Company, LLC

The 5R Journey
5R and 5R Journey are Trademarked by MaKelia D. Mitchell, Ph.D.

Published by The DOCMDM Publishing and Writing Works, LLC

DEDICATION

This book is dedicated to

My wonderful, loving and praying mother,

KATHIE L. WASHINGTON-MITCHELL

and to my beautiful, fierce, always supportive sister Monica R. Mitchell-Thomas; my handsome, wise nephew Mekhi N. Thomas; and to my sassy, fashion-forward, ever helpful niece, McKenzie R. Thomas

This book is also dedicated to my guardian angels who I am sure guide and protect me daily: Susan Pearl Washington, Elijah Mitchell, Sr., Elder Mary Fordham Mitchell, Deacon Leroy Mitchell, Sr. and Susan Renee' Washington-Nottage.

I LOVE AND APPRECIATE YOU ALL!!!

And most importantly, I dedicate this book to
GOD, MY LORD, SAVIOR, HEALER AND RESTORER, THANK YOU FOR THIS TRUE, THROUGH-STORY AND FOR USING ME AS YOUR VESSEL. I THANK AND PRAISE YOU FOR PRESERVING ME FOR SUCH A TIME AS THIS. I AM HUMBLED AND ETERNALLY GRATEFUL!!!

TABLE OF CONTENTS

FOREWORD

Jesus replied, "You don't understand what I'm doing now, but someday you will,'" (John 13:7, AMP). True transformation is often preceded by darkness, destruction and uncertainty. It is also mired in confusion, deficit and loneliness. Oh, but on the other side!!! On the other side, we get light, newness, and boldness! We receive clarity, triumph and fullness! And what I've witnessed in my good friend and sister in Christ, Dr. Kesha, has been a wonderful and glorious transformation! It hasn't been easy, as I've had to intercede and pray fervently on her behalf because I saw that she was following the enemy's path of destruction. I knew that God had a call and purpose on her life… but she couldn't yet see it and wasn't ready to truly surrender.

Through prayers and intercessions, I can now celebrate her victory and deliverance. Every text message, every conversation, every spoken affirmation, every silent prayer uttered was certainly not in vain! I have witnessed the metamorphosis. I have heard the testimony and the boldness in her voice. I have read the story of her redemption and restoration and can say without a doubt, "BUT GOD!"

This book is more than a cautionary tale; it's a story of how much God really loves and wants us. It's a song of why Christ died for us. It's a sweet melody of us truly not understanding how God in His power reclaims, removes, renames, resets, restores, readjusts, and redeems. Further this book is a manifestation of how much the heartfelt and persistent prayer of the people of God can accomplish much!

Let Kesha's story of faith and God's wonder-working power help you overcome whatever you are facing because

God is not one to show partiality to any of His children and desires that we should all be saved. The realness and rawness of her story and her 5R Journey makes me proud. As I continue to bear witness to her evolution and exponential growth, I will celebrate this triumph for years to come!

Dr. Kesha, THE BEST IS YET TO COME!

Sincerely,
Reverend Dr. Gerald Folsom

My suffering was good for me, for it taught me to pay
attention to your decrees
Psalm 119:71, NLT

True repentance is firm and constant, and makes us
war with the evil that is in us, not for a day or a week,
but without end and without intermission
John Calvin

I understood myself only after I destroyed myself. And
only in the process of fixing myself, did I know who I
truly was
Sade Andria Zabala

~And they have defeated him by the blood of the Lamb
and by their testimony. And they did not love their
lives so much that they were afraid to die.
Revelations 12:11, NLT

INTRODUCTION

The Parable of the Lost Son

Luke 15:11-32 New International Version (NIV)

[11]Jesus continued: "There was a man who had two sons. [12] The younger one said to his father, 'Father, give me my share of the estate.' So he divided his property between them.

[13] "Not long after that, the younger son got together all he had, set off for a distant country and there squandered his wealth in wild living. [14] After he had spent everything, there was a severe famine in that whole country, and he began to be in need. [15] So he went and hired himself out to a citizen of that country, who sent him to his fields to feed pigs. [16] He longed to fill his stomach with the pods that the pigs were eating, but no one gave him anything. [17] "When he came to his senses, he said, 'How many of my father's hired servants have food to spare, and here I am starving to death! [18] I will set out and go back to my father and say to him: Father, I have sinned against heaven and against you. [19] I am no longer worthy to be called your son; make me like one of your hired servants.' [20] So he got up and went to his father. "But while he was still a long way off, his father saw him and was filled with compassion for him; he ran to his son, threw his arms around him and kissed him. [21] "The son said to him, 'Father, I have sinned against heaven and against you. I am no longer worthy to be called your son.'[22] "But the father said to his servants, 'Quick! Bring the best

robe and put it on him. Put a ring on his finger and sandals on his feet. ²³ Bring the fattened calf and kill it. Let's have a feast and celebrate. ²⁴ For this son of mine was dead and is alive again; he was lost and is found.' So they began to celebrate. ²⁵ "Meanwhile, the older son was in the field. When he came near the house, he heard music and dancing. ²⁶ So he called one of the servants and asked him what was going on. ²⁷ 'Your brother has come,' he replied, 'and your father has killed the fattened calf because he has him back safe and sound.' ²⁸ "The older brother became angry and refused to go in. So his father went out and pleaded with him. ²⁹ But he answered his father, 'Look! All these years I've been slaving for you and never disobeyed your orders. Yet you never gave me even a young goat so I could celebrate with my friends. ³⁰ But when this son of yours who has squandered your property with prostitutes comes home, you kill the fattened calf for him!' ³¹ "'My son,' the father said, 'you are always with me, and everything I have is yours. ³² But we had to celebrate and be glad, because this brother of yours was dead and is alive again; he was lost and is found.'"

As I sit here today, I realize that I was truly a prodigal daughter who has returned home to her Father. Notice, I didn't say AM, I said WAS. This distinction is important because AM describes my present—where I am now; however, WAS represents my past and where I was. Being in a prodigal state means being wasteful, recklessly extravagant, (Webster's Dictionary) and when anyone is still in a prodigal state, they haven't yet realized that they need to be delivered and returned to their Father. When I say prodigal, I am not only referring to wasteful spending—I am also referring to spiritual resources, or any resource that helps you to succeed in life including time and health.

In this book, you will get the opportunity to learn about my journey. You will also have an opportunity to reflect and journal as you make your own way to redemption. It doesn't matter what issue you are facing! There is always a way back home.

I also offer a restorative prayer at the end of each chapter just in case you don't have the "right" words to say as you open your heart and spirit to hear the Father's call to you. If you seek true redemption and not just forgiveness, you are ready to be filled with the Holy Spirit as true redemption involves a change of heart and not just a change of behavior. Inviting the Spirit back into your life and heart serves to strengthen you and truly provide you with ALL that you need.

The Prodigal Daughter Returns will take you through my journey, my 5R journey and process - my true, through-story - of having almost everything and just about ending up with nothing. If I asked God for anything, it was because I felt I deserved it. Like the prodigal son, I lived riotously and recklessly and I almost squandered it ALL, before I finally come to myself and returned to my Father. I take no credit for the song of the redemption and restoration I'm able to now enjoy. I realize that I am still a work in progress and there will be constant evolution.

Let me inspire you with this even in your prodigal state; it is not too late to come to yourself and realize there is better. It is not too late to go your Father and seek His redemption. It is not too late to receive His divine restoration. He wants you to come to Him and will celebrate when you do!

HOW TO USE THIS THROUGH-STORY, PRAYER GUIDE AND RFLECTIVE JOURNAL QUESTIONS

- Each chapter begins with verses relative to the Parable of the Lost Son (Mark 15:11-32), which forms the basis for that chapter. Following the verses is a practical analysis, intertwined with my "through" story and journey. You will then be provided with reflection, thought provoking questions to help you examine your own life and journey. Finally, you will find a Scripture-inspired prayer designed for you to restore your relationship with our Father, a 5R Affirmation created so that you can begin to speak health, wealth and life over yourself. These affirmations should be spoken aloud as you make declarations of encouragement and self-empowerment to help you achieve success through your journey. There are other Scriptures provided for your reference as you continually delve deeper into God's word.

- Remember, this book and all that it contains are designed to assist you on YOUR journey of restoration and redemption, so feel free to:
- Read the chapters in chronological order as presented
- Reread as necessary, repeat each step or chapter as often as needed and jump ahead if you need to in order to be encouraged, inspired and reminded, as often as required to maintain a "right" relationship with our Father.
- Share the through-stories, prayers and affirmations with your entire circle!
- JOIN US!!! Go online to share your stories, testimonies, photos, videos, impressions, posts and tweets to

encourage, inspire and affirm each other on all social media platforms.

- Use the hashtags #myprodigalthroughstory and/or #my5Rjourney and tag us so that we can follow your story and provide any support you may need!!! (Please see back cover for links to follow us on all social media platforms).

CHAPTER 1

It's Mine! Give It to Me Because I Deserve It!

[12] The younger one said to his father, 'Father, give me my share of the estate.' So he divided his property between them.

So often, we are blessed by God and began to take those blessings for granted. For example, every flawless and effortless breath we take is a miracle as is every time a child is born. Yet, how often do we stop and take the time to say "thank you." We get a promotion on our jobs and instead of taking the time to be grateful and appreciate that in and of itself as the gift, we go out and obtain more and more things.

Why? Because we want and desire everything that we believe is ours NOW! We don't want to wait because after all, shouldn't we be enjoying right now the things we have worked for and that God has blessed us with? We take for granted that God will give us more and more simply because we ask. It is definitely true that God will supply all of our needs and bless us abundantly; however, we have to be under His arm of protection and not separated from him.

Deuteronomy 28:1-14 (NTL), more specifically verses 12 and 13 are often quoted as some of the blessings and benefits of God. Paraphrased, these verses contain the frequently quoted, "you will be the lender and not the borrower; you will be the head and not the tail; you will be on top and never the bottom." They even detail and outline all the ways that God will bless us. But we overlook the stipulation that is given in verses 1, 13 and 14—we must fully obey the Lord and carefully keep his commands; we must not turn away from any of them. We want the gifts but not the Giver. We expect to receive the rewards but not follow the rules.

As far back as I can remember, my life has been blessed and I knew that God's hand was on me. Don't get me wrong. I didn't have everything I wanted, and I even had financial struggles. However, God always provided and I had everything I needed and mostly everything I wanted. For instance, I was blessed with my first house at 23. I had multiple luxury cars, designer clothes, shoes and jewelry—all in my early twenties. I didn't consider myself to be living "riotously", but I was certainly irresponsible. I was so irresponsible that I applied for and received every credit and store charge card offered to me. I eventually overextended myself on each and every credit and charge card by living way above my means and ended up having to file Chapter 7 Bankruptcy. But God restored me and I got back everything that I lost and then some. I moved to a different city and began rebuilding.

When I finished my terminal degree, I thought to myself, "I'm good now—I have it all". God began to bless and prosper me in ways I couldn't imagine. My money, credit limits and access to funds exploded! I had multiple checking and saving accounts that were all "FAT". I could do and buy whatever I wanted, and trust me, I did. I asked God to prosper me, and HE DID! Metaphorically speaking, I asked Him to give me my share of the estate, and HE DID! He gave me more than I asked for or even deserved and in the end, it still wasn't enough.

In my mind, I was still severing God and had every intention of staying connected to him even after he blessed me. Admittedly, I wasn't fully committed nor obedient, but I felt I was doing just enough. I was active in my church, serving in differ-ent ministries and using my spiritual gifts. But, I was straying further and further away from Him. Why? Because I asked for my share of what he had for me. What I didn't realize was that asking for my share and beginning to drift further and further away from Him demonstrated that I had come to a mental and spiritual juncture that reflected an attitude of, "I have everything I need so I can just go my own way now". I'm getting ahead of myself a little, but that's exactly what happened to the prodigal son and that's exactly what happened to me—the prodigal daughter.

Let me pause here to explain that I didn't think my asking God for my share was wrong. I still don't think it's wrong. Our Father desires to see us prosper and He delights in giving us good gifts. However, we must realize the ramifications of having everything for which we've asked. For example, we should consider is we're mature enough to handle the blessing? Are we prepared enough? Are we truly sure we can handle everything that He has to give and we are asking with right motives and intentions? Let me tell you that I now know I wasn't. I wasn't ready the first time and I wasn't ready the second time. I wasn't seeking His will for my life and using all that He had given me for His glory. I wanted what I wanted because I believed I worked hard for it and deserved it. Crazy and wrong, right?

Where are you now? Are you asking God to give you your "share of His estate"? Are you asking Him to give you more than you can handle right now? Are you asking with right motives and intentions? Trust me, if you aren't, maybe you should ask God for an "allowance" and not necessarily your share. I now know I wasn't ready for my share. I wasn't ready for everything He had for me all at once - in my twenties nor in my early forties. The lesson I learned is that I was only ready for the allowance, not a gigantic share. I learned that I hadn't yet matured or prepared enough to handle and be a good steward over the blessings. I also learned that my motives and intentions for the blessings weren't honorable. They were selfish and used to gratify the desires of my human nature. And that only leads to destruction.

Reflection Questions

Take out your journal and a pen. Answer openly, honestly and completely.

1. What is the difference between asking God for your "allowance" versus asking Him for your "share"?

2. What would you do with your share if God did give it to you?

3. What makes you think you are ready to receive your share versus your allowance?

4. How does your level of stewardship reflect your readiness to receive your allowance?

Prayer

Heavenly Father, You promised to supply all of my needs according to your riches in glory and You know exactly what I need. When I ask You for anything, please search my heart and check my motives. If I am praying for anything that You know I can't handle, reveal it to me, Father. I desire to forever be in Your will. If my maturity and responsibility levels are not where they need to be to receive my "share," I ask that you prepare me to receive. Fill my heart with love for You and let me desire You above all material possessions. Teach me to seek You and Your kingdom first. In Jesus' name, AMEN

My First 5R Affirmation
I Will Be a Good Steward and Seek God First

I am a good steward of all that God has given me. Whatever is mine is ultimately His. I can do nothing without Him and I am nothing without Him. From this day forward, I will seek God in everything I do and will align my desires and motives to His will for my life. I will seek Him first and know that in putting Him first, all and everything He has for me will be added.

Additional Scriptural References

(Use the additional Scriptures as references to further your study and strengthen you on your journey.)

John 1:16	Proverbs 2
Proverbs 3:5-6	Psalm 25:1-5
Jeremiah 17:5-8	Matthew 25:14-30
2 Corinthians 4:4-7	Proverbs 9:1-6; 10-12
Psalm 27:1-6	Luke 12:42-48
1 Chronicles 29:17	Proverbs 3:9-10
Proverbs 21:2-3	Luke 6:38

CHAPTER 2

I Have Everything I Need and Want—Let the Living Begin!

¹³ *"Not long after that, the younger son got together all he had, set off for a distant country and there squandered his wealth in wild living,"*
(Mark 15:13, NLT)

You may recall that in Chapter 1, I contended that getting our share of an inheritance causes us to separate ourselves from our Father and His covering. Well, that's exactly what happens in verse 13. The prodigal son, not long after getting everything he asked for, decided that he should set off on his own and live how he wanted to live. As long as he was living with his father and under his protection, he was good. His father's house offered not only protection it offered guidance and direction. Of course there were probably rules of the house that governed behaviors but even those rules were in place for all the children's good. It was only after the prodigal son decided that he had everything he needed he could set out on his own and live how he wanted to. What was the consequence of his decision? He squandered EVERYTHING!

Like the prodigal son, I had money, credit and everything I needed and wanted. If I saw it, I bought it. If I wanted to eat out everyday, I did. If I wanted to drink everyday, I did. If I wanted to party every weekend, I did. If I wanted to buy all my friends drinks, I did. If I wanted to go to a club and buy sections and bottles, I did. If I wanted to travel wherever and whenever, I did. I figured, I have it, so I'm going to enjoy it. If I can pay my bills every month, I can do what I want. None of these things are wrong if you are using wisdom, exercising sound judgment and planning for the future. Life is to be enjoyed but it should be in the context of our Father's laws and commands. However, I took no thought that when I asked for and received my share and decided to separate myself and live apart from my Father, my share would be limited and eventually run out.

In describing the prodigal's spending habits and behaviors, the King James Version (KJV) notes, "he wasted his substance with riotous living, (Luke 15:13). I like the words wasted and riotous because to me, they really portray what the son had done and how he was living. He didn't save nor did he have a plan for tomorrow. He lived for the moment. He lived unrestrained, loosely and wantonly. He was partying and having fun! The scripture doesn't explicitly say this, but can only imagine that the prodigal, while parting and enjoying his life, was also treating his friends, eating wherever and however he wanted to and drinking as much as he wanted to. He was probably beginning to overindulge in many things such as alcohol that were in stark contrast to his upbringing, teachings and beliefs in his quest to enjoy his newfound freedom. Prior to his riotous and reckless phase, there were probably things that he never imagined doing. While he was out there, though, there were no limits or boundaries.

I can imply this from the scriptures because the same thing happened with me. Before my own riotous living, I avoided alcohol like the plague. In fact, I abhorred it, wouldn't even touch it because alcoholism runs in my family and I was determined not to let it happen to me. I don't think I had my first drink until I was 27!

When I did start drinking, I did so only socially and I was definitely a "light weight". I would drink mixed drinks or wine only and would never even think of drinking at home alone. However, as time went on and I felt that I could handle it, I drank more and more. As I got older and was going out more, I drank more. When I faced setbacks or disappointments, I drank more. As I started to sink into depression and was afraid to expose my weaknesses, I drank more. Eventually I switched to mixed drinks and graduated to straight alcohol and multiple shots. Drinking became an almost daily occurrence. Gradually, I started drinking at home alone—something that I vowed that I would NEVER do! I couldn't even see the downward spiral I was on nor did I recognize how my life was being affected in other ways.

Where my reputation was intact and pristine, it became tattered and torn. Where I was once regarded as a "queen" and above reproach, I became known as a drunk. I would get so drunk that I would stumble and fall in public.

Drunken, I had minor car accidents I couldn't remember where I parked my cars and would lose my keys. My friends would be afraid for me to drive home. I would miss work and other appointments because I was too hung over to show up where I needed to be. If I did manage to show up I would be late and often times still not be 100% there. I would make excuses and try to deflect attention from my growing alcoholism by trying to explain my tardiness, forgetfulness and absences.

How I was feeling and living was more important to me than anything else in my life at that point. I even pushed my family and friends away once it got really bad. And all of this happened and gradually escalated a little over a three-year period. Despite the embarrassing drunken stupors and humiliating escapades from being inebriated and hung over, I was still having fun and enjoying my share and couldn't see that I was sinking deeper and deeper and drifting further and further from who I really was.

I took no thought as to what I was doing to myself and to others. I never stopped to ponder how my living and lifestyle of today would affect my tomorrows. I was free to do what I pleased with my share. After all, my Father gave it to me so I could live how I wanted, right? I could still think about and thank my Father for providing for me. Since I wasn't living in His house, I could do what I wanted now, right?

As I examine my life in retrospect, I couldn't have been more wrong! Living how you want to and squandering all that you have will lead to death and destruction. I destroyed relationships and myself living riotously. I alienated those who were closest to me by living and behaving destructively. I lost almost all of my money and ruined my stellar credit by behaving recklessly and wantonly.

Maybe, at this very moment you are living recklessly and can't seem to stop the destructive behaviors. If it is, you have to stop right now because you are likely not living under your Father's covering and protection.

Rest assured, it will only be a matter of time before your share runs out as mine did. You will become the very thing you despise because you are using your share incorrectly and are enjoying your life. You will begin to think that this lifestyle will last forever. As someone who once lived recklessly and riotously, let me assure you that apart from God, your share will not last forever.

Reflection Questions

Take out your journal and a pen. Answer openly, honestly and completely.

1. Imagine yourself living apart from your Father. Describe, in as much detail as you can, what that might look and/or feel like.

2. In what ways are you currently living riotously?

3. What would steps would you take to assure that you are constantly connected to your Father?

Prayer

Father, I know that I am nothing apart from You because in You, I live, move and have my being. You are my source, my strength and my everything. Right now, I pray that I will always be connected to You, and even if I stray, please don't allow me to stray too far. Remind me that I need you and cannot live without your love and protection. In Jesus' name, Amen!

My Second 5R Affirmation

*I Will Stay Connected to My Father
and Live for Him*

I am a child of the Most High. In Him, I have an abundant life that is filled with blessings and everything I need. Living apart from my Father brings nothing but destruction and death—literally and figuratively. From this day forward, I will live with Him and will seek to do what pleases Him because with and in Him are fullness of joy, provision and protection.

Additional Scriptural References
(Use the additional scriptures as references to further your study and strengthen you on your journey.)

Ephesians 2:8-10	Psalm 84:15-22
Psalm 23	Exodus 15:2
Numbers 6:24-26	Psalm 18
1 Corinthians 6:19-20	Psalm 121
Psalm 68:1-20	Luke 12:22-32
Isaiah 43:1-4	Romans 8:31
Romans 6:23	Matthew 10:29-31
Psalm 5:4-6	

CHAPTER 3

What Do You Mean it's Gone?

¹⁴ After he had spent everything, there was a se-vere famine in that whole country, and he began to be in need. ¹⁵ So he went and hired himself out to a citizen of that country, who sent him to his fields to feed pigs. ¹⁶ He longed to fill his stomach with the pods that the pigs were eating, but no one gave him anything

So, here we are. The prodigal son had spent his entire share and a famine hit the distant country in which he decided to take up residence. My Bible doesn't say it, but in my mind's eye, the famine didn't happen in his father's country. Even if it did, the father would have ben wise enough to prepare for it and would have stored up enough provisions to last throughout the famine. Did you catch that? I'll come back to it for those who didn't! Anyway, a famine hit and he had nothing! His bank balance was ZERO. All of his credit cards were either maxed out or he could no longer afford the payments! He wasn't working, just partying and living it up; therefore, before his fall, he wasn't working and had no income. To make ends meet, he decided to get a job feeding pigs - something that was against his religion and beneath him as the son of a wealthy landowner. Again, my mind's eye shows me that his pride and fear of rejection kept him from going back to his father to ask for forgiveness and to be restored. I am sure he felt that what he had done was unforgiveable and that he deserved every bad thing that happened to him. After all, it was his fault, right?

Why can I believe that's what he was feeling at the moment? Because that's exactly how I felt when I lost almost everything while living recklessly. I condemned myself with thoughts like, "You did this to yourself and have nothing because of your actions. God is going to punish you so don't even ask for His forgiveness!" I was also thinking, "You will just have to suffer through this and find a way to make it on your own." My once fat bank accounts were all nearly empty! My credit cards, some of which had a $35,000 or more credit limits, were nearly to their limits. In other cases, I simply did not have enough money so I stopped paying the bills. I became physically ill and received a life-altering diagnosis of cancer followed by an undetermined autoimmune deficiency and could no longer work; so my income was greatly reduced as I survived off short-term disability payments.

Because I was out of work for an extended period of time due to being ill, my once six-figure salary was gone and my employers rightfully filled my position and required me to reapply once I could return. I hated my job anyway so I made the rash decision that I would never return even if I could.

In hindsight, I now realize that I wasn't just ill physically. I was also ill emotionally, mentally and spiritually which probably manifested into my physical aliments. But I really wasn't worried about that because I had my share of multiple savings accounts and credit cards that would sustain me until I could return to work or find another job, right? Wrong! I depleted my savings and couldn't keep up with the payments on my credit cards. I had eviction notices on my door. I totaled my car and I didn't have the means to get another one. I was down to nothing both literally and figuratively—no income, no money, no car, failing health and no hope.

You would think that being almost down to nothing would deter me from living riotously and recklessly. Any logical and rational person would try to change. At that point, that just wasn't me. I would still party, drink, mix a myriad of prescription drugs with alcohol and live as recklessly as ever. I felt that I didn't deserve better. I decided that if I was going to die anyway, I might as well go out with a bang. Most importantly, I was still too prideful to ask for help. "No one was gonna judge me," I thought. Even through the famine and working in a bar, I was reluctant to ask my Heavenly Father for help. Please don't get me wrong. There is absolutely nothing wrong with working in a bar! In my case, working in a bar was so far removed from my level of education, chosen career path and what I was called to do. It was what I settled for because I wasn't ready to completely surrender and return to my Father. I was content and ready to settle for whatever I could get because of fear and condemnation. On my own, I couldn't begin or attempt to make any significant changes. I was fully prepared to continue living against His plans and will for my life because of my desire to hide and do it my way.

When we are living apart from our Father, we are living outside His will for our lives. Earlier I said that I could imagine that the famine that hit where the son was didn't hit where the father was or impact his land in any way. Why? Because famine never hits our Father's land! He always has plenty and always has abundant provisions. All He has is perfected and protected. He never runs out of anything.

As soon as the son departed from his father, he lost his father's protection and provision. He lost the abundant flow and began to walk in the limited flow. I believe that with God, when we are living and walking according to his will for our lives, He provides for us abundantly, constantly and infinitely. However, when we are living outside of His will, what is provided is limited and finite. The problem with that is, when the "provided for" flow ends, there is no way to get more because your limited provision has been exhausted. But, God's constant flow is endless and again His provisions are limitless. We can't expect to live riot-ously in the land of plenty and not prepare for the time when the famine hits. Famine always hits. It might not be your finances or the material posses-sions that are attached to the famine.

It could be your relationships, your health, your life or the life of your family or the famine could be your relationship with the Father when you can't feel Him near. Whatever the circumstance, if you are connected to your Father, you will survive the famine because He will provide for you. You will live your life in a way that has you prepared for the famine so you will have more than you need.

Reflection Questions

Take out your journal and a pen. Answer openly, honestly and completely.

1. What have you squandered or surrendered while living riotously? Express how this makes you feel.

2. What would it take for you to get everything back on your won?

3. Describe how you are currently living. Is it a state that is "beneath" where God has called you? Why or why not?

4. How does living in famine feel?

Prayer

Father, I realize that I have squandered all that You have given me. I have lived riotously and apart from You and am not where You have destined me to be. My desire is to return to You. Father, forgive me for my poor choices and show me how to return to You and Your land. What You have for me is so much greater than anything I can ever want for myself and where You desire for me to be is infinitely better than where I am right now. Rescue me Father and lead me back to You. In Jesus' name, Amen!

My Third 5R Affirmation

I am on a Campaign for God and Will Cherish
Every Good and Perfect Gift

I am on a campaign to live for God and will not squander any financial, spiritual, material, mental or physical blessing that He has provided to me. Living in famine is a sin and dishonors God. It also discourages others who may see me from coming to Him. From this day forward, I will cherish and protect every good and perfect gift that comes from the Father of Lights and be an example of His grace, love and mercy.

Additional Scriptural References
(Use the additional scriptures as references to further your study and strengthen you on your journey.)

Psalm 73:21-28	Proverbs 1:2-4
John 15:5	Psalm 33:18-19
Psalm 89:5-18	Acts 17:28
Psalm 84:1-7	Romans 14:7-9
Psalm 84:8-12	Luke 11:11-13
Psalm 4:8-10	Matthew 5:3-11
James 1:16-18	

CHAPTER 4

"And then..." Can I Really be Redeemed?

[17] "When he came to his senses, he said, 'How many of my father's hired servants have food to spare, and here I am starving to death! [18] I will set out and go back to my father and say to him: Father, I have sinned against heaven and against you. [19] I am no longer worthy to be called your son; make me like one of your hired servants.'

These verses above clearly indicate that the prodigal son had an "and then" moment. An "and then" moment is when we receive a sudden realization. It's a moment that we get smacked upside the head with a thought that has always been there. We realize that there is and has always has been an answer. It' kind of like an "ah ha" moment. The prodigal son "comes to his senses (the ever-present realization) and thinks to himself, "I really don't have to live like this! I have a father who has everything. Maybe he will forgive me if I ask. I know I can't and don't' deserve to be his son again. Surely he will let me just work for him. If he lets me work for him, I will be fine." The prodigal son even imagined what he would say to his father and anticipated what his father's reaction would be. He was hoping and praying for redemption but didn't know if he would receive it. At this point, what could he lose by simply asking?

We cannot even begin to change our famine until we can first visualize a life of abundance. We cannot begin to change our circumstances until we are ready to admit that we need to be reclaimed and who can redeem us. The prodigal son's first thought was, "I don't have to live like this anymore." The he thought, "I know who I need to ask for help." The King James Version (KJV) says, "he came to himself," meaning that he finally realized who he was and whose he was.

He wasn't just a broke, hired field hand. He was the son of a father who lived in abundance. Therefore, he could return to where he belonged. He realized he could go back home! While he did not know if he would be received, he recognized that all he could do is ask. Maybe his father would turn him away.

On the other hand, maybe his father would take him back with some reservations and conditions. Maybe he might not be in the same position as a son, but he could at least be back with his father. He might have to start all over or even at the bottom; nevertheless, he would be back where he belonged in the first place had he not tried to live apart from his father.

While I had been praying half-heartedly in asking my Father to forgive and heal me, I was still living the same way and still hadn't completely surrendered. I was still drinking heavily and mixing prescription drugs with the alcohol. The little finances I had left went right into partying and having a good time. Other people would buy me drinks if I didn't have any money on me. At the time I wasn't strong enough to say "no." Why? Because I wasn't really repentant or ready to make any significant changes. I was still good with living in the pigpen and doing my own thing.

My pigpen was literal and figurative. I didn't care how I lived and my surroundings reflected that. If you saw me out, my hair and nails were always done. I still wore all designer clothes and shoes. I was always jeweled, make-up in tact and driving a Benz. However, I was living in what could only be described as a mountain of boxes and insignificant mess in a dark, dank basement.

When I stepped out, anyone who saw me wouldn't believe it because I always made sure I masked it and protected the façade at all costs. I wasn't even in my own house; but it didn't bother me! I was in the process of purchasing a home so I moved in with one of my closest friends until the sale went through. What should have been a temporary, six-months at the most stop, ended up lasting for almost two years. Honestly, I didn't even care about my surroundings. I ignored everything because living riotously was more important to me. In the course of living reck-lessly, I severely damaged and almost destroyed, one of my longest, closest friendships. I knew I needed to change, but wasn't ready. Honestly, I really didn't know how. Even when I did move into my own and changed my physical landscape, my mental landscape or way of thinking didn't change. My surroundings improved, my lifestyle didn't. Heck, I think it might have gotten worse. I wasn't just physically apart from my Father, I was totally apart from Him. I realized that it wasn't just where I was living or where I was physically, I was apart from Him spiritually, emotion-ally and mentally. I really knew I needed to make a change; I was just unsure as to how.

I started keeping a prayer journal on August 20, 2017, at 5:44AM because I am more expressive when I write. I tend to censor my thoughts and words when I speak; however, when I write, I let it flow and can go on forever. On that morning, I poured out my heart to God and told Him where I was spiritu-ally, mentally, financially and physically, though He already knew it all. I asked Him to help me and to forgive me. Quite honestly, I didn't really think He could or even would because I had brought such great loss and devastation upon myself. While I knew that God is able to forgive and would forgive, I still didn't forgive myself, nor did I make the wholesale changes to my life that were required. Every day and night, I wrote out devotions and affirmations. I wrote out my prayers. I asked for forgiveness. My mother and sister kept asking what I was writing and why I was writing so much. I wouldn't tell either one of them. I just kept writing and praying. I wrote out my prayers for two reasons. First, I write because I am an expressive person and writing comes naturally to me. Additionally, I found that I needed to write because I am "goal driven" and wanted to have a written "measurement" of my progress over time. I didn't know if I would ever see any progress; however, I knew I had to document my journey and the steps I had taken to heal and get better. (Little did I know that my prayer journal would morph into this testimony of redemption and restoration! See, God always has a plan for our lives that we don't always know or can't see. Us not being able to see it doesn't matter to Him. He will open our eyes and revel it to us in His divine and perfect timing). Although I started the prayer journal and poured out my heart in it all day and every night, I was still drinking and mixing prescription drugs with alcohol. In short, I had still not completely surrendered.

On September 10, 2017, the day before my birthday, I had a one-car collision in which I struck a guardrail. I totaled my car. I had been drinking and temporarily blacked out. To this day, I can't even remember the events that caused the accident. I had asked God for His forgiveness but wasn't ready to change my behaviors. I wanted God to change the situation but to leave me alone. I wanted to be absolved of every sin I had and offense I had committed without really repenting. How crazy! How could I even expect that to happen? It's because I was still living in the pigpen mentally and emotionally. On my birthday as the events from the night before and calls came in piecing together what has occurred, I began to reflect and think. I knew at the moment that God's hand was on me. I needed to change because I could have killed myself or someone else, or I could have been arrested. Despite knowing what could have been, I still entertained the notion that I didn't have to change all the way.

This is where we have to understand that there is a vast difference between forgiveness and repentance. To forgive means to grant pardon for or remission of an offence or to absolve of wrongdoing. According to Webster's Dictionary, to repent means to feel such sorrow for sin or a fault as to be disposed to change one's life for the better. Do you see the difference? To merely seek God's forgiveness means that you acknowledge you did something wrong and want Him to pardon or absolve you. However, when you repent, you want God's forgiveness, as you experience sorrow for the wrong you committed and realize that you need to change your life. Essentially you are confessing, "Father, I know I am wrong and have sinned against You. Please forgive me and turn my life around. I know I need Your help and can't change on my own. I want to live a life that is pleasing to You and ask You to change me right now." Now do you see the difference? If not, we'll take a closer look at the difference between the two in the next chapter.

On September 17, 2017, my pastor preached a message he titled "Shifts." I knew God was calling me to shift—to transfer my mindset from a place of dysfunction and addiction to a place of redemption and freedom. In the seven days prior to my pastor's message, I was receiving devotions and affirmations and words spoken over and into my life about how God was going to move and how He was going to bless and restore me. I was still drinking, by the way, when those words were spoken over me. I listened to each and every word but did not believe any of them.

October 4, 2017, was the day that I realized that while I was asking God to forgive me, I wasn't repentant, nor did I believe redemption could be possible for me. I also realized that I had not come to a place where I had I forgiven myself. I then realized that in order for me to be delivered, I needed to take those steps to get out of my pigpen. That entire day, I kept asking God for the courage and strength to forgive myself. I sought Scriptures about forgiveness and finally, repentance and redemption. I even reached out to one of my spiritual mothers about the spiritual and mental conflict I was experiencing. She sent me the following message.

My Love,

Ask yourself this questions, who am I not to forgive myself when my Creator, my Father, my Lord and King has forgiven me and extended His grace and mercy to be with me all the days of my life. Keep looking to the One you know never has nor ever will fail you. You must claim this forgiveness and know without a shadow of doubt that because of the blood of Jesus Christ, YOU ARE FORGIVEN. Now,

Daughter of the Most High, RISE UP and DON'T LOOK BACK! Take one step forward each day and each moment.

That's when I knew I had to ask God to bring me back to Him and not live in condemnation. I had my own "come to myself" moment October 5, 2017 at 12:05 am. That's when I prayed this prayer:

Dear Father,

I just want to say thank You. I know that I got my breakthrough today and I praise Your name for deliverance! I am free and forgiven because of Your blood. I never thought about forgiving myself before and I thank and praise You for placing that in my spirit. I truly believe that this is one of the keys to release all that You have for me. How can I receive if I'm walking in shame and condemnation? How can I receive if I don't believe I am worthy? How can I testify and witness to others when I am not bold or honest about all You've done for me? I just thank You for that, Father, and don't wanna belabor the point. I just love You, Lord, and know all things are working for my good. Time means nothing to You. You can move however and whenever you please.

Honestly Father, I think that's where this emotional instability was stemming from—I was so ashamed and condemned that I didn't feel worthy of your blessings. So, I would cry and doubt—NO MORE!!! I AM FREE!!!! Thank You for dropping this in my spirit Father!

You say in your word that we must never forget that a day is like a thousand years to You and a thousand years is like a day (2 Peter 3:8). I love you Father and trust and believe! You have me in the palm of Your hand. You will protect me and sustain me. Okay, no more! I love and thank You and praise You for washing me and now I can walk BOLDLY in ALL!

In Jesus' mighty name, AMEN!

I actually wrote that out in my prayer journal. It was at that exact moment that I realized I could return back to my Father, but only after forgiving myself. It was at that moment that I began thinking that repentance and redemption were even possible. I knew I might not be restored to where I was, but I was still His daughter. He would therefore place me where He wanted—even if I had to start at the bottom and just work for Him wherever He assigned. I had no expectations Only that my Father would forgive me.

Do you doubt that your Father will forgive you? Are you still in your pigpen? Have you "come to your-self"? If you have not, please know that as I finally learned, your Father is longing to forgive you. He is longing to deliver you from your pigpen. He gave you the desire to "come to yourself"; you just have to walk in it and act upon it. Our Father desires that none of His children perish. You are precious to Him and He loves you unconditionally.

I like to think that God has a perfect will and a permissive will. His perfect will is what He has purposed for and desires for all of our lives. His perfect will does allow for trials and tribulations to enter our lives because those make us strong and teach us to depend solely on Him for all. Conversely, His permissive will is what He allows to happen to us when we set ourselves apart from Him and decide to depart from His perfect will. He permits us to live in a pigpen. He permits us to become an alcoholic and hit rock bottom. He permits us to lose everything. His permissive will also teaches us, though those lessons are often harsher and much more difficult. If you are living in His permissive will, I implore you to "come to yourself" and live abundantly in His perfect will.

Reflection Questions

Take out your journal and a pen. Answer openly, honestly and completely.

1. Describe the pigpen in which you are living. (It could be mental, physical, spiritual and/or emotional).

2. What are some things that you may have done that you feel are unforgiveable? Why are they unforgivable?

3. How do you picture "coming to yourself"? Detail what that looks and feels like to you.

4. In your own words, describe God's perfect and permissive will for your life.

5. Do you believe you can completely forgive yourself for all you have done? What barriers still persist that you believe prevent you from accomplishing this?

6. Imagine completely forgiving yourself. How does

that look, sound and feel?

7. What is the difference between forgiveness and repentance? Do believe you need to ask God for His forgiveness or do you need to seek repentance? Explain.

8. Think about keeping a prayer or reflective journal. Would this be beneficial to your journey? Why or why not?

Prayer

Father, Your word teaches us that there is no condemnation in You and that You are faithful and just to forgive us when we ask. Because of these promises, I am confident that You forgive me. Father, teach me how to forgive myself. As I come to myself and begin to return to You, cleanse me of everything that would prevent me from living in Your prefect will. Create in me a pure heart and put a new and loyal spirit in me. I desire Your perfect not permissive will for my life and am ready to live fully for You. Thank You for delivering me from my pigpen and preparing me to walk fully and upright in You. In Jesus' name, Amen!

My Fourth 5R Affirmation

I AM Forgiven and Will NOT Live in Condemnation

The word of God promises that He is faithful and just to forgive us. If we confess our sins, He will cleanse us of us all unrighteousness. Because of this, I AM forgiven and will no longer live in condemnation. Nothing that I have done will cause me to not repent and return to God and live fully in Him. From this day forward, I will turn away from sin and live a life that pleases Him and intrigues others so much that they will want to know more about my Lord and Savior.

Additional Scriptural References
(Use the additional scriptures as references to further your study and strengthen you on your journey.)

Ecclesiastics 3:11	Psalm 34:4-7
Colossians 1:13	Jeremiah 31:34
James 4:8a	1John 1:5-10
John 4:34	Ecclesiastes 3:1-8
Psalm 69	Psalm 102
Matthew 19:26	Mark 11:22-24
Matthew 4:17	James 5:15-16
Psalm 142	Romans 8:28-30
Psalm 7-10	Romans 8:32-34
Psalm 25:6-22	Numbers 14:18
Psalm 5:1-3	Psalm 33:20-22
Luke 11:9-10	Psalm 51
Jeremiah 14:14	Psalm 103:12

CHAPTER 5

Yes, You Have to Make the First Step and Be Contrite

²⁰ So he got up and went to his father. "But while he was still a long way off, his father saw him and was filled with compassion for him; he ran to his son, threw his arms around him and kissed him. 21 "The son said to him, 'Father, 1 have sinned against heaven and against you. 1 am no longer worthy to be called your son.

Once the prodigal son "came to himself" and decided he would no longer live in a pigpen but return and be restored to his father, he had to take the first step and make the first move! While his father may have been praying for him the whole time, he couldn't just go get his son. He had to let his son make the first move and return to him. While he was glad to see his son and even greeted him with an embrace and kiss, his son had to admit his wrongdoings and shortcomings. He had to admit that, because of his desire to leave his father and live apart from him, he needed to confess his sins, ask for forgiveness, admit the fact that he was not worthy of redemption and prepare to hear whatever judgment his father was ready to proclaim.

I can imagine the prodigal son holding his head down and saying, "Father, I am so not worthy to be called your son because I've wasted what you've given me and have lived a life that is contrary to all you have taught me. I can't even tell you some of the things I've done. Although I am your son, I've debased myself and have made myself common—not princely as is really my inheritance." I can also imagine the father standing there listening, with tears streaming down his face, shaking his head back and forth because he knew all his son had done and was just happy to have him back before anything happened to prevent their reconciliation.

Why are those images so easy for me to illustrate for you? Because, I felt exactly the same as the son when I decided to return to my Father. That boy's posture was precisely as my own.

On October 7, 2017, I began to return to worship, and I began a fast. I started to fast because I knew I had to do something different in order to have the deep, meaningful and life-changing encounter I needed with God. I needed to be completely empty so that He could fill me. I needed to be free from all distractions so that I could hear His voice. I needed be fed spiritually and not just physically. I had to get in a posture in which I was completely surrendered and hungry. I was hungry not for physical nourishment, but for spiritually nourishment. I was ready to hear Him, feel His presence and be filled by His Spirit. This is what I wrote in my prayer journal:

Dear Father,

Thank You for this day! Thank You for your many blessings. I am truly grateful for every single, solitary moment of this day and all You've allowed me to see, hear and do! I am forever blessed and prosperous because of Your grace and mercy. I only have my being and mental faculties because of Your loving-kindness. Lord, thank You for forgiving me and allowing me another opportunity to get it right. Father, I love You and worship You. Not only for what You've done but for who You are. Father, You are magnificent. You are awesome. You are King of kings and Lord of lords. You are my Rose of Sharron, my Lily of the Valley, my bright and morning star. Father, You are The Most High, my everything, my all and all. You are my sword and shield, my strength, my buckler. You are Alpha and Omega—my beginning and ending. There is none like You! No one else can touch, heal or fill me like You do! I worship You with every fiber of my being! I bow to You, my sovereign Lord! You are excellent and all together perfect! You are matchless, and You reign supreme. I can do nothing without You! My heart, soul and my body belong to You.

Father, today, I am beginning a fast. My fast is not intended to ask You to grant my every desire as a genie in a bottle. It is solely intended to draw me near to You so that I may hear Your direction. It is to change me, not You or Your heart. It is to grant me clarity so that I will know which way to go. It is to worship You and sacrifice what little I have to give to honor You. Father, I ask that You consecrate this fast and that it be pleasing in Your sight.

Lord, I dedicate this fast to You and offer it to You that it may be a sweet smelling fragrance to You. Father, from today, Friday to Monday morning, I will only consume fruits, vegetables and water. If I stumble, I ask that You convict my spirit so that I may be corrected. Like Queen Esther (Esther 4), I want my fast to bring You honor and glory and that it be pleasing to You. If You can do it for Esther, You can do it for me! If You could do it then, You can do it now! Please accept this offering and may it be pleasing to You. Favor and directions are my only motives for this fast and if those motives are wrong, please forgive me. Father, show me the right way. I want to be pleasing to You.

Bless my fast O Lord and move the mountains that exist in my mind, body and soul on my behalf. May the words of my mouth and the meditations of my heart be acceptable in Your sight, O Lord, my strength and redeemer.

In Jesus' name, AMEN!

At this point I had returned to my Father and asked for His forgiveness. I knew I needed to be prepared to listen, hear and accept whatever He had to say. I had to prepare to be redeemed by Him, even if that meant that I had to lose everything I had, even my idea and concept of self. Even if I would no longer be a leader or a respected for what I had attained and start all over, it had to be done. I had to approach my Father with a broken spirit and contrite heart.

During my fast, God spoke and revealed Himself to me anew. I received prophetic proclamations, affirmations and encouraging messages like, "this is your season of restoration"; "God still loves, heals and He still restores"; "prepare yourself, for I am about to take you to another level in your life"; "TRUST GOD"; and "God hears your every prayer". These prophecies gave me strength and encouragement, though I knew I wasn't quite there.

It was also at this point that I had to determine whether I was simply asking God to forgive me, or was I ready to truly repent? We have already established that there is a distinct difference between forgiveness and repentance. Just based upon the definitions, forgiveness means to grant pardon for or remission of an offence or to absolve while repentance means to feel such sorrow for sin or fault as to be disposed to change one's life for the better.

Forgiveness, to me, means saying, "I'm sorry, my bad, I didn't mean for that to happen." And when we ask for forgiveness, we kinda have it in the back of our minds that, "while I'm sorry this happened, it just might happen again and I'm fine with that." Conversely, when we repent, we are taking a posture of, "Father, I really messed up this time and know that my continued mess ups are leading me to think this might be acceptable, when in fact, it is not. Father, I need your help to make a wholesale change to my life and make every effort to not repeat these behaviors. If I do repeat them, convict my spirit right away so that I can repent immediately." Does God forgive you when you ask? Of course He does - He even promises that He "will remove our sins as far from us as the east is from the west (Psalm 103:12, NLT). But when we repent, we are vowing to turn away from and stop our "detestable sins" and get back in to a right relationship with God.

Although all sin separates us from God, we receive forgiveness when we ask for it. Not only do we receive grace that forgives, when we repent, our relationship with Him is restored. Keep in mind that when we repent, we admit that we have done something detestable that requires a deeper level of contriteness and restoration. To seriously change, I knew I needed to repent in order to hear from God and receive His.

To show that I seriously wanted to change, I asked, no, I begged God to lead and guide me to the Scriptures I needed to read and exactly what I needed to see. In granting my request, God gave me the books of Hosea and Genesis 32 and 33. For those of you who don't know about the purpose of the book of Hosea, let me give you a brief history as recorded by The New international Version of the Bible (1984):

Through his own experience of a broken marriage Hosea gained a deep insight into Israel's relationship to God. The covenant made at Sinai was like a marriage, but like Hosea's wife, Israel had left God to worship Canaanite gods. Hosea speaks movingly of the sadness God feels because of his love for Israel even though she deserves to be punished.

In other words, just as Hosea's wife was adulterous and continued to leave him to pursue other men; Israel did likewise by pursuing other gods and idols. Though Israel sinned and deserved God's punishment and "divorce", God still loved them and longed to forgive them. How appropriate and relevant to my current situation, I thought! I have sinned continually against God and made everything else in my life a god and really deserved for Him to abandon me. Yet, He didn't! God should have divorced me for committing adultery, but He still loved me and wanted me back!

After gleaning those nuggets in Hosea about how God was willing to forgive me, I began to study Genesis 32 and 33. In these chapters, we meet Jacob as he is preparing to be reunited with his brother Esau for what he thought would be judgment and punishment. You see, Jacob had tricked his brother Esau out of his birthright and all that came with it. Once Esau found out what Jacob had done, he vowed to kill him. Consequently, Jacob ran away upon hearing the threat of death.

So at this point, Jacob knows that he had sinned against his brother and was preparing to meet Esau's wrath and receive his well-deserved castigation. And I'd say that Jacob deserved it! Wouldn't you agree? Understandably, Jacob began to pray and ask God for deliverance. Even in doing that - seeking God and asking for deliverance - he still had a plan to trick Esau. Ever the trickster, Jacob was not committed to fully asking for forgiveness of his brother and trusting God's perfect plan. Once Jacob did fully commit to sinning no more and giving God all, an angel was sent to him. He stayed up all night wrestling with the angel and declared, "I won't let go until you bless my soul!" The angel sent by God, blessed Jacob and changed his name from supplanter and trickster to Israel—one who has prevailed with God. Through that wrestling match, Jacob was left with a limp, a permanent reminder of his struggle for redemption and blessing. Jacob then meets Esau and is forgiven and blessed, not punished or cursed! In similar fashion, when we surrender completely and return to God, He will forgive us and bless us beyond our wildest imagination!

Here's what I applied to my life from the book of Hosea and Genesis 32 and 33:

1. I am the "harlot" whom God has married and is constantly begging me to turn from my adulterous ways.

2. My husband, God, still loves me and longs for me to be His faithful bride.

3. God, even through punishment, desires for me to be faithful and committed to Him.

4. Even after punishment, God loves me and wants to redeem, restore and bless me.

5. This is my opportunity to return to God and depend solely upon Him, even though I don't

deserve His care.

6. I cannot manipulate God into blessing me.

7. God must be my only source [of everything].

8. I need to examine my prayers so that even when I'm praying and seeking God's plan for my life, I am not trying to be manipulative.

9. God owes me NOTHING!

10. I can't pacify God with half-hearted attempts to return to Him and ask for forgiveness.

11. My prayers have to show total dependence on God.

12. Even when God forgives me, I will have a permanent reminder of His redemption and blessing.

13. Am I ready to die than to live without God and His blessing, even if it means losing everything?

14. God can restore me, but even if He doesn't, He's still God and is still good.

15. Even as I prepare to receive punishment and correction, God still favors me!

Isn't that powerful? God longs for us to be in right-relationship with Him and even when we are apart from Him, His love is constant and He will restore us once we repent!

After my nightlong study of the book of Hosea and Genesis 32 and 33, I began to pray on October 8, 2017, to thank God for new revelation of familiar passages of scriptures. This was my prayer at 2:12:

Father,

Thank you for divine connections and direction! Thank you for leading me to the book of Hosea and to Genesis 32 and 33. Like Jacob, I won't let go until you bless my soul! Father, thank for changing my song of praise! Father, my names used to be liar, cheater, drunk, manipulator, user, fake, a harlot, lazy, late, sneaky and deceptive. But after wrestling with You, I have been redeemed and you have changed my name! I am now the Daughter of the Most High! I will walk in my new name and shed those of my past! Father, I am still wrestling and am determined not let go until you fully and continually bless my soul!

Yes and Amen in Jesus' name, AMEN.

Right after I wrote that prayer and declaration, I read a devotional from my Bible app that stated, "You are a new creature in Christ. The old you is gone. You don't have to answer to that old name again!" Isn't that divine confirmation?! You see, through my fast, God changed the very nature of who I was. I was finally returning to Him and becoming all that He destined me to be.

On October 8, 2017, at 2:45 am, this is what I wrote in my prayer journal:

Father,

I thank and praise You for this day! Thank You for ministering to me and speaking to my heart. Thank You for divine visitation and our "wrestling match" last night! Thank You for blessing my soul! Like Jacob, I wrestled with You and you've blessed me and changed my name! I am now The Daughter of the Most High!!! Father, thank You for confirming Your prophetic words this morning! I know that word was for me and it seals everything that You and I have talked about. I love You for Your heart, Father, and want more of You! Father, as I begin Day 3, the final day of my fast, I consecrate and dedicate it to You! Again, Father, give me right motives and desires. Give me a new perspective as I continue to seek You. Continue to speak to my heart, giving me direction. You are my light and my salvation. In You do I place my trust and have my being. I expect an even greater encounter with You today.

In Jesus' name, AMEN!

Later that day, I went to visit another church. The topic of the message there was "Reset". All I could think was WOW!!! I then attended a Sunday jazz brunch that featured live gospel artists and one of the songs that was performed was "Changed" by Tramaine Hawkins. If you aren't familiar, I implore you to listen! The theme of the song conveys the complete and profound change that God has provided. It details how the Savior, once we allow Him to, comes into our lives and changes the way we think, walk and talk. I counted none of this as coincidence but looked at every event that occurred during that weekend as God confirming His words to me.

I took each sign of confirmation as a new covenant between God and myself and began to embrace my new, changed name and identity. On October 9, 2017, at 12:15am, this is what I wrote in my prayer journal:

I declare that God has:
1. Reclaimed me
2. Renamed me
3. Reset me
4. Restored me (In progress, happening even now)
5. Renewed me (on going…The Prodigal Daughter)

(I call these my 5Rs)

Through my fasting and praying:
1. I had a divine visitation from God.
2. I felt my spirit completely change.
3. I felt the Holy Spirit enter my life.
4. I am being rebuilt.

Through my fasting and praying, I learned:
1. I have to totally consecrate myself and set myself apart (I can't be in social situations and still hear from and communion with God. I am not strong enough yet.)
2. I am not strong enough yet to ever depend on myself.
3. I have to totally depend on God.

Through fasting and praying:
1. I pray that I pleased God, and He honors my sacrifice.
2. I pray that I have forever been changed.
3. I pray that my growth will be sustained and

increased exponentially. I continued to pray and worship God in words and through songs as I mediated on all that I had gone through and the transformation that had taken place in my life. As I meditated, I desired to cement my commitment and revelations and epiphanies in a way that would allow me to memorialize all that I had learned. At 3:45am, I wrote:

Father,

I have prayed verbally to you and have been speaking with you all day so I won't belabor that point. I'm just so thankful for you speaking to me and sending me confirming prophetic messages. From our prayer time, my fast and the prophetic words, this is what I've learned:

1. I AM the prodigal daughter who has returned to the outstretched arms of her Father!
2. Since it has been prophesied that this is my season of breakthrough, maybe the first breakthrough had to be a spiritual one.
3. Maybe my financial, employment and other breakthroughs had to come AFTER the spiritual one.
4. There is not going to be one singular breakthrough—this is a SEASON and I will experience MULTIPLE and CONTINUOUS breakthroughs.
5. You have spoken to me—I have to learn to hear and follow Your directions and instructions.
6. I have to start having a verbal dialogue with

You and not just use my prayer journal—this leads to You speaking to me as I verbally pour out my heart to You

7. You know my every need and they WILL be supplied according to Your riches in glory.

8. I am made whole in and because of You and have to stop beating myself up when I fail because I will, but you still love and will forgive me.

9. You always provide correction.

10. Your love for me is unmatched and You love me with an everlasting love.

11. I long for your approval and long to know that I am pleasing you.

12. I WILL NOT be defined by my past! You have reclaimed and renamed me!

THANK YOU, MY SWEET HEAVENLY FATHER!!!

I know and realize that was a lot. I simply wanted to reveal how God changed me and how I came to identify myself as the prodigal daughter. You see, I had to return to my Father and ask him to reclaim me as His servant.

I knew what the Bible says about God's love and forgiveness but had never experienced that type of life-changing encounter. What I could have never known without that encounter was that God had been waiting and looking for me and was ready to welcome me with rejoicing, tears and kisses. He was ready and waiting for me! I don't know about you, but that gives me chills.

The Most High waits for His prodigal children to come home, and He rejoices when we do. And how do I know He is looking for and waiting on us?

The Scripture uses the analogy of the prodigal son and his return to his father. Mark 15:20 tells us that, "…while he was still a long way off, his father saw him and was filled with compassion for him." That means his father was on the constant lookout for his son as he spotted him from a long way off. The son didn't even make it all the way to his father's doorstep before he ran out to meet him!

I learned and am saying to you right now that our heavenly Father does the SAME THING!!! When He sees that we have made the first step to return to Him, He has compassion and blesses us IMMEDIATELY with open arms and kisses! I made the first step and experienced God's compassion, sweet embrace and loving kisses. Will you do the same and make the first step back to your Father?

Reflection Questions

Take out your journal and a pen. Answer openly, honestly and completely.

1. What does having a contrite heart mean to you?

2. Describe how you imagine God's reaction will be when you return to Him.

3. What steps would you need to take to begin a spiritual fast? How would you need to prepare mentally, spiritually and physically?

4. What could be the possible benefits of your fast?

5. List the first 3 steps you need to make to return to your Father? What would that look, feel and sound like?

Prayer

Father God, in the name of Jesus, I am tired! I am truly tired of living apart from You and going my own way. Father, I am taking this first step back to You. I want to be near You and can't live without You. I know I deserve Your wrath and punishment and am ready for whatever correction you have to administer because I know you only chastise those who you love. However, I know You are a loving and compassionate Father. Have mercy on me, Father, and cover me in your warm embrace. Show me what I need to do to be close to you again. Speak to my heart and heal me. I am broken and need You to repair me. Change me now Father and cover me with Your love. In Jesus' name, Amen!

My Fifth 5R Affirmation
God's Correction is ALWAYS for My Good

My Father longs for me to be in right relationship with Him and uses His punishment to correct and teach me everything I need to know. Even when he corrects me, it is done lovingly and serves to draw me closer to Him. No punishment He metes out compares to what I actually deserve. I am loved and cherished and will continually seek ways in which to become closer to Him. From this day forward, my mind, body, soul and actions will honor the love my Father has for me.

Additional Scriptural References
(Use the additional scriptures as references to further your study and strengthen you on your journey.)

Matthews 28:20	Job 5:17-27
Hebrews 13:5	Proverbs 3:11-12
Esther 4	John 15:13
Esther 5	Psalm 51:15-17
Psalm 119:67	Psalm 34:14-18
Psalm 6:9	Isaiah 57:15
Joel 2:12-14	Hebrews 12:5-11
1 Peter 2:21-25	Psalm 30:5
Psalm 139:4	Psalm 37:23-24
Psalm 33:18-19	Zechariah 9:12

CHAPTER 6

Restoration Leads to Celebration

²² "But the father said to his servants, 'Quick! Bring the best robe and put it on him. Put a ring on his finger and sandals on his feet. 23 Bring the fattened calf and kill it. Let's have a feast and celebrate. 24 For this son of mine was dead and is alive again; he was lost and is found.' So they began to celebrate.

Can you imagine the son's shock and surprise at his father's reaction to his return? He had to be standing there with a bewildered look on his face but tears running flowing from his eyes. He had to be thinking, "I don't deserve any of this! See, I came here expecting to be punished and chastised. I expected to be stripped of everything and treated like a lowly servant. I expected to have to work hard to regain my father's trust and favor again. I thought I would have to grovel and beg to get back into my father's good graces and receive his mercy." I shutter to think it, but I bet most of us who are parents would punish our children—if even for a short period of time—to teach them a lesson. And even if we welcomed them back, we would take a "wait and see approach" to determine if they would try to repeat the same behavior. We would have to be sure that they deserved our love, grace, mercy and forgiveness.

But our heavenly Father isn't like man. He deserves praise for that alone! He frets over His lost children and rejoices when we finally "come to ourselves" and return to Him. He watches and waits for any inkling that we are on our way back to Him. He also knows all that we had suffered while living riotously and in complete sin. He knows what we've lost and what we've done. We may try to hide from man, but God knows all, sees all and STILL welcomes us with "the best robe, ring and sandals". He is ready to stage a celebration and feast when we come back to Him because He realizes that we were dead but are now alive in Him. We were lost but are now found safely back on His land.

Before I returned to God and experienced His welcoming compassion and embrace, I felt like Jacob and the prodigal son. I expected harsh punishment and that it would take years for God to forgive me. After all, I had spent almost three years living riotously and recklessly. I had spent all I had and done everything but the right thing. I mean, I had lost almost everything and didn't have anything to show for my Father giving me "my share". I was a mess, a wretch, a total disaster. Despite it all, God still welcomed me. Was I now perfect? Absolutely NOT!!! I still messed up and still sinned against Him and STILL mess up and sin daily. I still struggled and still DO struggle to obey Him. But, I can thank Him and praise Him because He's never let me get that far again and I vow to never live apart from Him ever again. I vow to never let any thing or anyone get me that far away from my Daddy. In Him there is reclamation. In Him there is renaming. In Him, there is still resetting. In Him, there is restoration. In Him, there is still redemption. These are what I call my 5Rs—reclaiming, remaining, resetting, restoring and redeeming.

When I returned to God, He began to complete the 5Rs in and over my life. I believe the father gave his son a robe, ring and sandals for a specific reason. I also believe they represent exactly what God wants to do to us when we return to Him. The robe represents His holy covering. The father said, "Quick! Bring the best robe and put it on him" (Mark 15:22). The father had to put a robe on his son to show that he was covered or blanketed in protection and love.

I also imagine that the robe was specific to that family. Maybe it was a certain color, like purple, because purple represented that family and anyone who saw it would have to recognize that the son belonged to that family. Maybe it had the family crest embroidered on it. Again, that insignia or crest represented that family and by it, they would be recognized immediately.

I believe God does the same thing! He covers us with HIS robe that is a specific color and has His insignia so that everyone will now know that you're back with your Father where you belong! The ring represents His "marriage" or joining to Him. Again the Father said, "Put a ring on his finger" (Mark 15:22). This was a special ring—a ring that identified the son as "belonging" to the father. And the father didn't just say give him a ring. He said, "Put a ring on his finger." When someone "puts a ring on it," they are claiming you and saying to everyone, "Don't touch or even approach because this one belongs to me!"

God puts a ring on our finger to show that we are His and we belong to Him. And guess what, He doesn't want anyone to touch! Finally, the sandals represent that we are covered from the crowns of our heads to the soles of our feet! And these weren't any ordinary sandals. They had to be special for the father to place them on his son's feet. Maybe they also represent divine favor over everywhere the son would tread. The father says, "Put sandals on his feet". Our heavenly Father also places special shoes on our feet when we return to Him. He covers use from head to sole and blesses and protects everywhere we walk. He wants the world to see what He has done for us.

The father commanded his servants to "Kill the fatted calf" (the best one) and prepare a celebratory feast. He wanted everyone to know that his dead, lost son was now alive and found. He rejoiced because he didn't know if or when his son would "come to himself" and return home. But I believe he prayed, fasted, waited and watched until it came to pass. The father must have been confident after fasting and praying that his son would eventually return. I mean, if he wasn't confident, why would he watch and wait? Why would he anticipate his son's return if he wasn't confident that God had heard and honored his payers?

We only wait with expectation and anticipation when we are certain that what we have asked for is on the way to us. I am fully convinced that our Father does the same for us! He knows we have chosen to leave Him and He even allows it. He also knows that even in your being apart from Him, your detour has an expiration date ordained and set by Him. Even in your pigpen, He speaks to you and let's you know you need to return to Him. In my riotous living, God showed me, spoke to me, poked me and even prodded me to return, but I ignored every warning. God showed me that I was becoming an alcoholic and abusing prescription medication.

He even had my mother and some of my close friends say it to me. But you guessed it—I ignored them all. I would even get angry and indignant, like, "Man, I'm grown and I'm good." I even said to my sweet, precious mother whenever we were together and she complained about my behavior, "Leave me alone and just leave if you don't like what I'm doing!"

I felt that I could hide it from everyone and I could manage. He showed me that I was spending too much money and that I needed to slow down. Did I?

NOPE!!! I kept right on going and lost almost all of it. Just like my earthly mother, my heavenly Father was praying for me and watching and waiting for me to come back to Him. And when I did, I believe all of heaven threw a Holy Ghost party for me! I believe my Father was like, "Finally, Hard Head!" I believe He covered me, remarried me and protected my feet.

Has God fully restored me and given me back everything I lost? Nope, not yet; however, I firmly and fully believe He will, VERY SOON and it is being manifested in my life EVEN NOW!

I do believe and trust that God put a robe on my back, a ring on my finger and sandals on my feet the instant I decided I would return to Him. He immediately performed the 5Rs in my life the second I "came to myself", and he saw me coming from a distance. I know that I have already been reclaimed, renamed and reset. My earthly restoration and redemption are being released and are happening each day!

I have prepared myself for the marathon and not the race because my restoration and redemption will be a forever process for me. It will always be the "thorn in my side" or a war wound of the battle in which I had to actively assist in fighting for my life. I know that with every fiber of my being I must trust my Father's divine timing. His timing is perfect and His promises are always true. Wherever you are in your prodigal or 5R journey with God, trust that He is working all things together for your good and is going to provide you with a tsunami type blessing. What He has decreed and declared in Heaven will be made manifest on earth.

If you have returned to God, but haven't yet seen the earthly manifestation of your robe, ring or sandals, I implore you to not give up and go back to the pigpen! Stay in your Father's land and wait on Him. He hasn't delivered or brought you this far just to leave you where you currently are and He is working all out behind the scenes.

Reflection Questions

Take out your journal and a pen. Answer openly, honestly and completely.

1. What have you anticipated to be God's reaction to your return to Him? Detail your feelings.

2. Where would you place yourself on the 5R journey with God? Why?

3. What would it take to get you to the next step/phase of your journey?

4. What steps do you need to take to get there?

Prayer

Father, O how You love me! Thank You Father for Your love and forgiveness. Thank You for celebrating at my return and rejoicing that I am back in Your arms. Thank You for my robe, my ring and my sandals. Thank You for covering each and every part of me. Father, I thank You for reclaiming, renaming, resetting, restoring and redeeming me. I have left the pigpen and ask You to help me to never return. I am ready to receive all that You have prepared for me and wait in anticipation for Your many blessings. In, Jesus' name, Amen!

My Sixth 5R Affirmation

I am Built for the Marathon with God

My Father always desires for me to admit my short-comings and failures to Him so that He can continually perform the 5Rs in my life. This is a marathon, not a sprint or short race and I am prepared to seek Him at every phase—reclaiming, renaming, resetting, restoring or redeeming—and will repeat any and all phases as necessary. From this day forward, I will do whatever it takes to stay in right relationship and fellowship with Him so that others will see the glory of God through my life.

Additional Scriptural References
(Use the additional Scriptures as references to further your study and strengthen you on your journey.)

Psalm 119:17	Isaiah 53:4-6
Jeremiah 1:52	Joel 2:20b-21
Corinthians 4:8-10	Matthew 18:19-20
Psalm 27:11-14	Matthew 18:11-14
Psalm 119:44	Luke 15:4-7
Colossians 6:13-14	Luke 15:8-10
Ezekiel 34:11-16	Philippians 1:6
Lamentations 3:22-23	Romans 8:31-39

CHAPTER 7

Yes, Others Have Endured Hurt and Pain While You Were Living Riotously

[25] "Meanwhile, the older son was in the field. When he came near the house, he heard music and dancing. [26] So he called one of the servants and asked him what was going on. [27] 'Your brother has come,' he replied, 'and your father has killed the fattened calf because he has him back safe and sound.' [28] "The older brother became angry and refused to go in. So his father went out and pleaded with him. [29] But he answered his father, 'Look! All these years I've been slaving for you and never disobeyed your orders. Yet you never gave me even a young goat so I could celebrate with my friends. [30] But when this son of yours who has

squandered your property with prostitutes comes home, you kill the fattened calf for him!'

When reading this parable, it is easy to forget or overlook the fact that the father had a second son. We forget because he was briefly introduced; however, up until verse 25, he isn't mentioned anymore. I believe this happens for two profound reasons. First, the older brother remains loyal and faithful to the father. Secondly, the father always had his eyes on him. Do I think the father forgot about him? Absolutely not! He just knew that "if my older son gets in to trouble, I can immediately recognize it and rectify it because he is with me always."

The older brother returns from his loyal, constant hard work, he hears the celebration and wants to know what's happening. I mean, no one even came to get him to let him know there was a party happening! I am sure he was hurt, angry and disappointed all at the same time. He probably thought to himself, "Nah, y'all have your little party! I wasn't invited and don't even know why y'all are making a big deal about this fool that came back home." He flat out refused to go in. But why would he? The father instantly recognized and acknowledged his oldest son's feeling and wanted to explain to him why this was, in deed, a BIG DEAL!

Was the older brother jealous? Sure, a little. Was he angry? Of this, I am sure! But I believe the most prominent emotions he felt were hurt and neglect. He was hurt that even though he had never left his father's side and had never sinned against his father, there were never any celebrations for him. He exclaims, in what I am sure was an exasperated tone, "'Look! All these years I've been slaving for you and never disobeyed your orders. Yet you never gave me even a young goat so I could celebrate with my friends. But when this son of yours who has squandered your property with prostitutes comes home, you kill the fattened calf for him!'" (Mark 15:29-30).

That demonstrates to me that he was hurt and felt neglected because his father never threw him a party. He spoke negatively about his brother out of hurt, even though the things he said were true. I can only imagine that the older brother talked and complained about his younger brother to his friends and the servants who were near. I'm also certain that he had to endure hearing other people talking negatively about his younger brother. That led to anger, resentment and hurt. He had to endure all of that, and now he had to endure the indignity of his father throwing a party for "this son of yours who has squandered your property..." The nerve!

I can fully relate to that. I had some very close friends who, out of concern for my behavior began talking about me. They witnessed the downward spiral first-hand and had every right to be worried about me. And trust, me, I don't blame them for their concern nor do I begrudge anything that was said. I tried to hide from them and didn't communicate my feelings to any of them even though I considered them my brothers and sister—but they knew all because I couldn't hide from people who really knew me. But guess what, I was hurt when I heard that they talked about me and not to me. I'm not sure I would have even been in position to hear them because I hadn't returned to my Father. I am certain I would have completely disregarded their words because I had become a master of keeping everything bottled up and being the strong one who didn't need anyone. I felt that I had to do everything on my own and on the oft chance that I did ask for help or an opinion, I wasn't going to receive it.

It wasn't until some of my brothers had the courage to speak directly to me about my out-of-control drinking and behavior. Previously, I mentioned that my mother had already said something to me. I'm also sure, that like the father in this parable, she prayed, fasted watched and waited for my return. I am more than certain she celebrated and threw her own praise party when she saw me coming back and finally admitted to her that I had a problem and was taking steps to fix it. But I'm flesh of my mother's flesh and bone of her bone—she kinda HAS to love me, right? However, my brothers and sisters don't— biological or not.

Even though I know they did and still do, they were disappointed with my behavior. They were hurt and angry that they had to hear other people talking badly about me because there was no way they could defend or refute the claims and stories because in all actuality, they were almost always true. While some of the murmuring, gossip and tales were untrue, when you establish a pattern of behaviors, how can anyone distinguish fact from fiction? Even when I declared to my Father and my brothers and sisters that I was changing and was coming back; I still fell and messed up. My Father continued to rejoicing because He and I were working on me behind the scenes. On the other hand, my brothers and sisters only saw that I messed up again, so they didn't want to celebrate. I now understand their hurt and frustrations. I understand the pain that my actions caused. I understand why they didn't "come get me and confront me." I am grateful for the confrontations that did occur and for the prayers that were said over and for me. I place no blame. Rather, I understand why they didn't get why my Father was throwing a party for my return. What I am grateful for is my Father entreating and "pleading" with them to come in and celebrate where I was in my journey!

No matter what's going on in your life, know that your being absent from the "family", whomever they are to you, has caused hurt and resentment. You have disappointed some people who loved and admired before you were living riotously in your pigpen. You have put them in positions where they've had to listen to folks making disparaging comments about you but couldn't even defend you because they knew most of it was true! Know that while they may still love you, they are human and don't have the same love for you that your Father does. Know that they want to celebrate with you, but have a hard time because they still see that while you are a work in progress, you will still have struggles. I implore you not to give up on or despise them! Keep being restored and redeemed and allow your brothers and sisters the opportunity to vent to you about you. They have endured much for you and want the best for you. They are only hurt and angry because they know what you were and what you can still be. As humans, we sometimes forget that even once our Father has started our 5R process, we will stumble and fall. Our Father loves us like no other, so He'll still dust you off and celebrate your return to Him as often as He needs to and as long as you can admit that you need His love and constant forgiveness!

Reflection Questions

Take out your journal and a pen. Answer openly, honestly and completely.

1. Who have you hurt while living riotously? (Name them specifically)

2. Imagine the pain, hurt and disappointment your actions have caused. How do you think they may have or still feel?

3. You've made the steps to return to God. Now make the steps to return to those you have hurt. List the steps you need to take.

4. Prepare a written apology to those you may have hurt.

Prayer

Father, I thank You even now, for speaking to my heart. I thank You for revealing to me those who I may have hurt while I was apart from You. I ask You to forgive me for hurting them and ask that You give me the courage to face them and ask for their forgiveness. I pray that You will give them a heart made of flesh and not of stone as I make apologies so that that they will receive my sincere words . Allow me to open my heart to hear what they have to say and use it to be better. Father, I ask You to help me restore any relationships that I have broken and I ask that they too, begin to celebrate my return. Father, repair my broken relationships even now and envelop us with Your love. In Jesus' name, Amen.

My Seventh 5R Affirmation

I will Build Right Relationships with My Brothers and Sisters

I live in right relationships with my brothers and sisters and will do what it takes to seek their forgiveness when I am wrong and/or cause pain. My brothers and sisters and friends love me and desire the best for me and I know that it is God's desire for us to live harmoniously with each other here on earth. From this day forward, my life of repentance will include seeking it from my brothers and sisters so that our relationships can bring honor to God and demonstrate His love for us all.

Additional Scriptural References

(Use the additional scriptures as references to further your study and strengthen you on your journey.)

Proverbs 28:13	Ephesians 4:32
2 Corinthians 4:1-1-2	Colossians 3:13
Proverbs 18:24	Mark 11:25-26
Romans 14:10-12	Luke 6:36-37
Matthew 18:16-17; 21-35	John 15:12
Luke 17:1-4	James 5:16
1 John 3:14-17	1 John 4:7-12
Luke 6:41-42	Luke 11:5-8
1 John 4:19-21	Proverbs 17:17
Matthew 5:21-24	
Proverbs 12:22	

CHAPTER 8

Let Your Father Intercede and Exhort Others on Your Behalf

31 "'My son,' the father said, 'you are always with me, and everything I have is yours. 32 But we had to celebrate and be glad, because this brother of yours was dead and is alive again; he was lost and is found.'"

Our heavenly Father loves and cares for us so much that He will intercede with others and plead with them on our behalf. As we come to the end of the parable, the father is explaining to his oldest son why he is celebrating his brother and why he has never thrown a party for him. Again, in my mind's eye, I can see the father with both hands on his older son's shoulders looking at him lovingly and squarely in the eyes. He's pleading with him to come celebrate his younger brother's return. The father explains to him that any time he wanted a party all he had to do was ask! Since he never left his father, everything, including the fatted calf belonged to him, too! He could have thrown a party every day of the week for all the father cared because he had twenty-four hour, seven-day a week access to everything the father had.

Conversely, the younger brother was lost and dead but is now found and alive. This was great cause for celebration because the brother was being restored and the family was being reunited. Of course the Bible doesn't include this, but I believe the brother begrudgingly entered the party and smiled once he saw his younger brother. I believe once he saw him, he was glad he didn't lose him and rejoiced that he had his sibling back by his side. I want to believe that he embraced his brother, just as the father had and maybe even lovingly punched his brother on the arm as he may have once done prior to the his departure from the family.

This is great news! Our Father will plead with others to accept you and implore them to forgive and embrace you. He will explain to them why there is cause for celebration and beg them to come and celebrate with you. I rejoice in that and praise my Father for doing this on my behalf, even now. I know that in my riotous, pigpen living, I hurt others and disregarded their feelings. I know that I alienated some family, friends and colleagues and discounted how much they loved me and wanted to see me win. I realize that I pushed people away because I wanted to continue doing whatever I wanted to and didn't want to hear their judgments or listen to their disappointment. I was ashamed and embarrassed to admit that I - the successful, driven and determined one - had a serious problem and didn't know how to ask for help. I didn't know how to say that I had let drinking and abusing prescription medication, and overspending ruin my life.

I didn't know how to reach out and express that I was disappointed and discouraged because getting the next job, position, house, car or relationship wasn't happening as quickly as I thought it should.

I was terrified to admit that I was scared due to the medical diagnosis I had received and considered ending my life because I felt it was over anyway. I either limited the amount of time I spent with those who cared deeply about me or I stopped associating with them altogether. I knew I was accountable to them even as I lived in squalor and ruined myself. I didn't want to face condemnation from them, the same way I felt that my Father was condemning me. Unlike my Father, once I confessed my sins and returned to Him, there was no more condemnation. I cannot say the same for some family and friends. They condemned me with their tongues and continue to do so until this day.

All I can do at this point is to ask them for forgiveness as I as I have asked and received from my Father. All I can do is urge them to come to my celebration because we have much to celebrate. Our Father has reclaimed, renamed, reset, restored and redeemed me! And even though I may slip and stumble, I will never be cast out because our Father holds me in the palms of his hands. I am far from and will never be perfect (despite my always thinking that I have to be perfect and live up to my own faulty expectations). My God has is still performing the 5Rs in my life, which means more than ever, and I need my accountability partners at this point in my life!

Realize where you are in your journey back to our Father. To me, that is the first step. Like the prodigal son, you to have to "come to yourself" and realize that you don't have to stay where you are. Your Father has more than enough and wants you to come running back to Him.

He prays for you, waits for you and watches for your return. He nudges you, even while you are apart from him to tell you to come back home. He wants you to come to back to Him. Your Father is ready to reclaim and rename you, but you must make the first step. You have to start walking back to Him.

Once you make that first step, you have to be ready for whatever He has for you. It could be punishment and correction. More than likely it will be a warm, loving embrace and tears of joy. While you are in His embrace and returned to Him, fast and pray so that you can REALLY hear and feel Him because it is then, and only then that He can reset you and place you on the "righteous" path. Lean your ear to His mouth so that He can speak to you. Let Him clothe you in His robe of glory, place His marriage ring on your finger and strap on your feet the sandals that will lead to trailblazing discoveries. He will then begin to restore and redeem you. He is ready to celebrate you and your return. Allow Him to cover you! Come back to Him, prodigal son or daughter and watch Him transform your life! Because He did it for me, I am confident He will. If He can do it for me, I am confident He will do it for you! Start wherever you are in whatever circumstance you may find yourself. It may be a long, arduous task. All you have to do is take the first step. I implore you my brother or sister, start now and come back home TODAY!!!!

Reflection Questions

Take out your journal and a pen. Answer openly, honestly and completely.

1. Who do you need God to intercede with on your behalf? Name them specifically and write what you would say if you could use God's voice to speak to them.

2. Where are you now on your 5R journey? Are there barriers or blocks that a preventing you from moving forward? What are they and how can you overcome and continue to move forward?

3. If you could plan the celebration of your return, describe who you would invite and what all it would contain. (Would there be music, balloons, food, etc.?)

4. I receive complete reclamation, renaming, resetting, restoring and redemption TODAY by _____.

5. List three to five ways you can receive the 5Rs and describe how this first step makes you feel.

Prayer

Father, I love and praise you for returning me back to You! I thank You for not allowing me to perish in my pigpen. I thank You that the call You have on my life is stronger than anything that is apart from You. Thank You for breaking strongholds in my life and delivering me from wherever or whatever my pigpen might be. You know my struggles, but you also know my potential. You knew me before I was in my mother's womb and the plans you have for me are awesome. I thank You even now that not only are you restoring me, you are restoring my relationships with my family, friends and all who I may have hurt while going my own way. Prepare the celebration for all my loved ones as I am back with you and receive your reclamation, renaming, resetting, restoring and redemption. In Jesus' name, Amen!

My Eighth 5R Affirmation

*My Interactions and Relationships with My
Brothers and Sisters Will Reflect the Love God
Has for Me*

I am on a campaign to live a life that pleases my Father. I will restore and maintain relationships with my brothers and sisters because those relationships influence others' perceptions of Christ-like families. I will seek to always be transparent and honest with those who love me. I will and ask for help when I am feeling lost, isolated, scared or discouraged because I can never do this life or accomplish my God-given purpose alone. From this day forward, my life will be a representation of a son/daughter of God who honors Him in words, actions, thoughts and deeds.

Additional Scripture to References
(Use the additional scriptures as references to further your study and strengthen you on your journey.)

Job 22:21-30	1 Timothy 2:4-6
Romans 12:1-2	Romans 8:26-27
1 Peter 5:10	Romans 8:35-39
Ecclesiastes 3:11a	Romans 11:1a-2
Ephesians 2:10	Titus 2:11-15
James 1:19-24	Romans 6
Psalm 126	Matthew 5:12-16
Luke 6:43-45	Matthew 5:42-48
Philippians 2:3-18	Luke 6:27-37

AFTERWORD

It is my sincere prayer and hope that this song of restoration and redemption blesses you and your life in some way. This is my journey and it has been a very difficult one. Alcoholism, prescription drug abuse or overspending may not be your struggle as they were and may continue to be for me.

Maybe you aren't even struggling right now. What I do know is that I have lived riotously and am now fully committed to never returning to a pigpen EVER AGAIN! Will I still sin and struggle? Will I still slip and fall? Might there be another issue that arises? The answer to each of those questions is a resounding YES! But at this point, I can be confident that my Father didn't take me through what I went through for nothing. He didn't strip and break me so that I could stay that way. He has truly rescued me and performed the 5Rs in my life. He has opened my life to a whole new set of possibilities and opportunities. One of which may be to try and help others see a way out.

The hardest part of this journey has been actually admitting that I was in a pigpen in the first place. Once I finally admitted to myself what others could see, I knew that I could change. Nothing was done by my might and I take no credit for my redemption. I know and fully recognize that it was the prayers of my beautiful earthly mother and my magnificent, matchless heavenly Father. It was the intercessory prayers of my biological sister and my adopted brothers and sisters. I know it was friends who may not have known exactly what was wrong, but they recognized that I wasn't myself. I even acknowledge the prayers of strangers who, when they saw me at my lowest, offered a simple, "Lord, have mercy." Because of all those prayers, love and constant support, I AM BACK, better than ever.

Putting this journey to paper has been cathartic, scary and freeing all at once. I am a very private person, so exposing myself in this manner is no easy feat; however, I know it had to be done. It had to be done for me to really be delivered because now, neither the enemy nor any man can use my past against me. It had to be done so that I could really heal and see how far my Father has brought me. It had to be done so that I, along with everyone in my life, could have a reminder as to why we have cause to celebrate my return. But most importantly, I had to be transparent because I truly believe that my journey and testimony is going to help inspire and deliver someone else. I didn't go through a pigpen just for my benefit—my pigpen is going to help someone else.

I naturally struggle in silence. It's just who I am. I feel that I have to always be strong and perfect. I now see and fully believe that these faulty thoughts and assumptions contributed to me entering in and even staying in my pigpen for as long as I did. I never reached out for help. I actually turned it down when it was offered. I was used to being a high achiever and being blessed with success early on in life. Subsequently, when I tried to switch careers, buy another

house or attempted new relationships and was reject-
ed or told to wait, I became disappointed and despon-
dent. In turn, disappointment and despondence
turned in to depression and resentment. My illness
compounded that depression and resentment. To
cope, I retreated and drinking and partying more. I
call it being unintentionally or unconsciously suicid-
al. I never planned on nor did it seriously enter my
mind to end my life but I had reached a point where
I didn't care if I lived or died. If I drank as much
alcohol as I could, took a handful of pills and slept
for the rest of my life, I wouldn't have cared. I didn't
have a healthy outlet, nor did I admit to or express
my feelings to myself or anyone else. Again, I wanted
to present the image of having it all together and
being on top. That all lead to secrecy, seclusion and
a self-imposed isolation as I thought I could handle
everything on my own.

I am geographically separated from my mother;
however, she knew something was wrong and wanted
me to come back home where she could take care of
me. Though I did return home to be with her for
an extended period of time, I hadn't yet returned
to my heavenly Father. I know I needed to let her
help me heal—not just physically—but emotionally,
mentally and spiritually. Still, I didn't want to "disap-
point" her by admitting that I had failed and didn't
even know how to cry out to her for help. I reveal all
this to convey that, even when our earthly parents
and family are praying for us and want us back with
them, we MUST first return to our Father to receive

full restoration. Take heed to the warnings and calls from your earthly family, but know, that you MUST go through your heavenly Father first. Please, seek outside, professional help and support if that is what is needed to get you through! I did that as well and there is no shame or harm in seeking professional counsel or therapy or even treatment programs or groups. Whatever it takes, you must do the necessary work and be committed to making the changes within!

Wherever you are and whatever you are going through, please know that your Father is waiting on you. Please know that He is ready for you to come home and live abundantly in Him. Also know that that you should forgive yourself because He certainly will. God and your earthly family are waiting on you. It's not too late! Come to yourself, make the first step and go back to your Father. Ask Him to forgive you. Ask Him to show you the steps to take. My own involved the 5Rs—reclamation, renaming, resetting, restoring and redeeming. Yours might be something totally different. Whatever the steps are, get up and GO!!! We are all waiting to party with you and celebrate your triumphant return!!!!

ACKNOWLEDGEMENTS

This is the part of any project that I AVOID writing because I always forget to include individuals who have definitely impacted me in some way. So, if I do inadvertently omit your name, please blame my faulty head and not my heart!

With that said, I'd like to acknowledge my father, Elijah Mitchell, Jr., who gave me life and teaches me more about life and how to treat others than he will ever know. Mr. Joseph Washington, Sr., my last living grandparent must also be acknowledged. He is one of the first examples of restoration and deliverance that I have ever witnessed and he always provides wisdom and a good laugh when I need one! To my brothers, Jamar Washington and Mark Thomas, I could never have made some of the hard decisions I had too if it weren't for your examples and advice. I'd also like to acknowledge my large, loveable extended family that includes the Mitchells, Washingtons, Greens, and Fordhams (and all other surnames added by marriage, adoption and those claimed off waivers).

I would also like to recognize my church families and more specifically my spiritual fathers, mothers, brothers and sisters—Pastor Keith Battle, Pastor Claudia B. Walter and Rev. Dr. Gerald Folsom.

My "Regal Beagle Crew" (S. A., D. D., K. G., S. L., K. R., T. R., D. S., I. S., M. T., and R. W.,), who are now and forever more my family members, must be acknowledged for their love, support and for confronting me when I needed it. Some of you even served as critics, early editors and cheerleaders! Whenever I struggle or need support, I know that I can count on you all to still pull me through. I wouldn't have been able nor can I continue to make it without you guys!

Of course I can't forget my host of friends who have become family (you all are too innumerable to name!), my social media family and my amazing support system! I must also acknowledge my writing coach, mentor and cheerleader Tressa "Azarel" Smallwood and her entire team for pushing me to get this done as soon as I could. To my team of editors, design and layout artists, photographer, graphic designer and web-based media team, I appreciate you for putting up with my last-minute changes, second-guessing and indecisiveness.

Finally, I MUST acknowledge some of very special "friendmily" (friends + family) members: T.C., C.M., Z.M., and M. A. You guys treated me, this book/story like it was your baby too. You prayed for it, nurtured it, made strategic and divine connections for it, and made sure I didn't quit—even when I thought it wouldn't be worth it. In my BEST SINGING voice, I'm screaming, "You mean the world to me, you are my everything!"

I LOVE AND APPRECIATE YOU ALL WITH MY WHOLE HEART AND ENTIRE BEING!
MDM